A GLOSSARY OF CHICKENS

PRINCETON SERIES OF CONTEMPORARY POETS

Paul Muldoon, *series editor*

For other titles in the Princeton Series of Contemporary Poets see page 58

A GLOSSARY OF CHICKENS

Poems

Gary J. Whitehead

PRINCETON UNIVERSITY PRESS
Princeton & Oxford

Copyright © 2013 by Princeton University Press

Published by Princeton University Press, 41 William Street,
Princeton, New Jersey 08540

In the United Kingdom: Princeton University Press, 6 Oxford Street,
Woodstock, Oxfordshire OX20 1TW

press.princeton.edu

Jacket art: *Two Chickens*, Milton Avery, 1948. Courtesy of the Hirshhorn Museum
and Sculpture Garden, Smithsonian Institution, The Joseph H. Hirshhorn Bequest,
1981. Photography by Lee Stalsworth.

All Rights Reserved

LIBRARY OF CONGRESS CATALOGING-IN-PUBLICATION DATA

Whitehead, Gary J.

  A glossary of chickens : poems / Gary J. Whitehead.—1st ed.

      p. cm. — (Princeton series of contemporary poets)

  ISBN 978-0-691-15745-0 (acid-free paper) — ISBN 978-0-691-15746-7

      (pbk. : acid-free paper)

  I. Title.

  PS3623.H5834G56 2013

  811'.6—dc2   2012032581

British Library Cataloging-in-Publication Data is available

This book has been composed in Adobe Garamond and Scala

Printed on acid-free paper. ∞

Printed in the United States of America

10 9 8 7 6 5 4 3 2 1

Contents

III

A GLOSSARY OF CHICKENS

OYSTER

Oyster I am and of course am not,
crammed betimes abed,
awake now and filter the world!

Here, in this wet
section, sucking away unread,
slaked where silt has quarreled

with silt, the as-yet
with now instead
of then, what has it availed

to live the clam, all shut
and somewhat dead,
all abductor-muscled,

flexed for no one but
yourself in your unlit head?
O, open! Be befooled,

three-chambered heart
full of colorless blood,
sharp shell unhandselled.

Better to be rent apart,
all jiggly and liberated,
than to fret an irk until it's pearled.

I

THE WIMP

They called me The Wimp, and I was.
Not for any reason I can put my finger on
but because, in general, I lacked wherewithal,

I was a poltroon, and none of them
knew that word or any better than "wimp"
and probably they still don't. If one of them does,

I wouldn't know so. Those years before
and during and after high school
swirl in my memory now like squalls of snow,

like the time when, on a whim, in late December,
my friends and I told our folks we were going camping
in the wildlife refuge two towns over,

the flakes already falling, our gear pitiful
hand-me-downs, none of it insulated or waterproof,
rum bottles clinking in our knapsacks like muffled toasts

to the end of our young lives. Inches had fallen
by the time we bivouacked at the Caratunk cave.
Wet kindling whispered. Not even leaves would catch.

In five o'clock dark, we crawled into the tent
soaked and shivering and stoned, no one willing to state
the obvious—that we might die out there in what,

we all knew by then, was a blizzard unpredicted.
Who it was had the wherewithal to suggest
we pack it in, I don't recall, but I remember humping,

drunk and exhausted, through two-foot drifts
in the hushed woods, my toes gone numb in thin boots,
our flashlight beams a mixup mystification

panning over moguls of snow-covered brush.
I wouldn't have minded expiring there
under the laden arms of a spruce.

The past is a distance, and life has, at times,
been a stumbling through thick drifts, batteries dying.
They'd think of me still as The Wimp.

So there's the future, like the lost pair of sneakers
we found in the spring, and growing between
their double-knotted laces a sapling.

LOT'S WIFE

Sometime soon after the embers cooled,
after dust clouds settled, after the last strings
of smoke, hoisted by desert breezes, cleared the air,

they must have come, people of those three cities
remaining, to pick among the charred bones,
the rubble of what was once temple and house,

stable and brothel; to kick at stones; to tug
at handles of buckets, blades of shovels and spades.
Later, raising ash plumes in the scorched plain,

cloths at their mouths and noses, eyes burning,
neither fearful nor repentant but full of wonder,
full of the scavenger's overabundant hope,

they would have found her—even as now
some men encounter the woman of their dreams
(beauty of the movie screen, princess they capture

with a camera's flash, girl whose finger brushes theirs
when she takes their card at the market register)—
found her, that is, not as the person she was

but as whom they needed her to be, and, man or woman,
each of them would have wanted a piece of her.
Standing in that wasted landscape,

she must have seemed a statue erected there
as a tribute to human frailty, white, crystallized,
her head turned back as if in longing to be the girl

she had been in the city she had known.
And they must have stood there, as we do,
a bit awestruck, taking her in for a time,

and then, with chisel and knife, spike and buckle,
chipped at her violently and stuffed their leathern
pouches full of her common salt, salt with which

to season for a while their meat, their daily bread.

SPICE RACK

It was the last thing I packed,
its fake oak and three-ounce jars
tacky with fingerprints—
olive oil, syrup and grape jam.

A wedding present, perhaps,
or a gift at Christmas
for the young couple we were,
its garlic salt, onion powder, cayenne

like ground-up charms
against a marriage too bland.
No one told us that spice
has a shelf life, that thyme,

like its homophone, is best
served fresh, that cloves
are good for nothing but hams.
Why, when she left,

she didn't claim it
I can only guess, but later,
cooking alone in a rented cabin,
I was glad to have it,

those neatly arranged
containers of pulverized seeds
and dried leaves. Celery salt
on eggs, curry on cottage cheese,

its stained and sticky base:
these made it easier to know
that, with her various lovers,
she was eating at tables more grand.

SOURDOUGH

Mother dough, seed sour,
flour and water.

Always the need to make,
even in hours

of slaughter or of want—
a dusted board,

cordwood in a tin bin,
an oven's heated maw.

To feed, to eat, to procreate.
Bread is perpetual,

is the gunk stuck in a thin
gold band,

the aroma crawling through
kitchen quarters,

the old and the new world
order.

Mother dough, seed sour,
flour and water.

The noun is my son,
the verb is my daughter.

LUMINESCENT JELLYFISH

Under the mainmast of the *Morgan*,
in damp Mystic dark,
I watched worms of green light,

fuses of the sea, lamps for small fishes
along the changing avenues of shallows,
and thought about the difference

between lust and love,
what some creatures will do
out of whatever it is that drives them.

I know I drove once through dense fog
to meet my lover,
the bridge I needed to cross

like a cloud inside a chasm,
and all I could see were two green lights
blinking, Gatsbian.

Not just the body, then, electric,
but the dream with its chambered tides,
that different desire and its gaps

which would be lit, its channels,
its many eyes: the unrealizable certainty
of the way things should be.

I'm sure I crossed that span,
or one like it, and that time hurried darkly
below what would've been a long fall.

I imagine there were gulls there, too,
unseen and shrieking. In truth,
I was probably hoping for nothing

of the kind, nothing more ideal
than the salty heat of her,
the deep, piqued plunge of a jellied oblivion.

Years later, beneath the tarry smell of the rigging,
leaning over the gunwale, I wondered
what those subaqueous flarings could teach me

that I didn't already know.
The body lives, after all, to glow.

SOMEBODY THROWS IT IN

Each day I fill the kettle,
click a knob for a blue flame.

Down at the river, another
ebb delivers drift—twigs

and branches, plywood
and other lumber, dozens of sizes,

all of it smoothed at the edge,
lighter than you'd expect.

None of us wants news
that's bad if it has to do

with us, the ones we love.
It exists at a distance,

but we know it's out there,
pulled by something like a sea.

Tragedy's baptismal.
I make coffee in the morning;

in the afternoon, tea.
On my walk, I see campers

using driftwood for kindling,
pyramids ablaze.

My brother Michael,
two hundred miles away,

can't stop thinking,
even in his sleep, about cells

building within him,
flotsam in the lymph.

He showers, takes drives
to get his mind off things.

The driftwood comes
from somewhere upriver.

Somebody throws it in.
It must be heavier then.

You'd never guess
it spent days in the river,

light as it is to lift
when the water has left it,

readily as it burns
after a day in the summer sun.

THE SLIP

No one I know will die today.
The sun will rise and spread
its bright net in the east.
There will be coffee or juice.
Some eggs, a double yolk
if I'm lucky, no bead of blood,
no gritty bits of shell.
The milk won't be sour
beyond its expiration date.
Neither will the tap drip
nor the marble counter chip
when I bang it with my plate.
In the shower, the lump I feel
will be the beginning
of a pimple, nothing more,
and the fear will flake away
like scrubbed skin.
My dog will eat and drink
and do his business in the yard,
another day closer to ten.
And so on and so on,
nothing, really, to report—
no funny sounding call
from family or friends,
no flat tire on the commute
from work, not even a drop
of the rain they predicted.
And I won't even be happy
to have slipped the net
when the sun sets in the west
with its dark and heavy haul.

TRAP DOOR

through which, like a fisherman's hole
in an iced lake, we sink into senselessness;
or through which, as a magician does,
we make our exit, the audience aghast,
the footlights burning on in the close room;

trap door through which all our lives
we imagine ourselves dropping
even as those we love trip the trigger
and vanish with their soft forms;

a trap because it catches us unawares
the way a snare a hare
or glue the whiskered snout
of a mouse in a dark larder;

a door because it lets us in as well as out;
and if, like the leaf-covered portal
of an underground fort
in a wood we thought we knew,
we cannot find it in our traipsing;

or if, like a hatch to a belfry
in which a swung bell beckons the penitents
of a small town, we need to reach
for some collapsible ladder;

and if the way to enter the attic
in the home of another's love;
if the way to the basement where a father taps
in radio code banal greetings across oceans;

if for a fall into what we knew
before we knew to know it;
for escaping tiled floors, shady lanes,
roads, mossy hills, building ledges,
or any gravitational plane;

then perhaps the last breath
a kind of latch, and whatever desperate
disparateness sensed looming
flung out like hatchery feed
to be nibbled by little mouths of relief,
the way my toes, dipped in a warm lake,
were kissed by sunfish once,
or the way, as a baby, one's tonsure
makes the rounds like a communal cup,
the warm, unformed gourd
just fallen through the first door;

and if that plummet a plummet back
to the unmade self before birth,
then each antecedent breath an ethereal rung
we release until we swim again
in the lake made for us.

Mother, by your mother's deathbed,
all night long, ice tapping at the windows,
the song of her dying like a wind across a gap,
and knowing how in her going
she clung to the edge,

how did you endure, afterward,
the water glass on the nightstand
with its ridiculous ring,
the alarm clock's red-lined numbers,
the bookmarked book,
the baseboard ticking?

And when you sleep in that very bed,
nights when your asthma drives you there,
do you, in your unsettlement,
feel for a trap door's seams
in the still air of that dim-lit room?

It is not the disappearance of the dead I grieve
but the way the living abscond
into the past, which is a kind of heaven,
into a distance, the way my mother,
sitting across from me, chews chicken with rice
but tastes the dish her mother made,

or the way, scratching the belly of my old terrier,
I see him again as a pup
running in his colorless dream,
or the way my brothers have vanished
from my day-to-day and I from theirs—

I fall into every Christmas
as into a manhole uncovered,
into a summer barbecue
as into a sinkhole in a backyard,
and my brothers, there as if to catch me,
do not catch me but high-five,
a congratulation for having landed
once more upon their separate lives.

On the stage of this my life, the days,
pulled like tied kerchiefs
from the black hat of what's next,
consistent with their knots,
offer little to hold onto,

and when the trigger trips
and the floor falls out from under,
with what wonder will I watch
the bright and patterned silk
pour like water with all that soft applause?

OWL PELLET I SHOW MY STUDENTS

This gray loaf full of tiny bones,
a gift I found on a park road,
like something a car drove over—
once mouse or mole but now
a skeleton sewed into one
undigestible measure.

No more than half an ounce,
this used-to-be whiskered skitterer,
who once engaged in nocturnal pleasure.
Not so unlike you,
reckless, reckless youth:
scapula, fibula, tibia.

What is it that surrounds all these bones?
In truth, I cannot say,
just as I cannot say what will one day,
under its caped wings,
gulp *you* down whole,
my soft little mousies, my tender moles.

ONE-LEGGED PIGEON

In a flock on Market,
just below Union Square,
the last to land
and standing a little canted,
it teetered—I want to say now
though it's hardly true—
like Ahab toward the starboard
and regarded me
with blood-red eyes.
We all lose something,
though that day
I hadn't lost a thing.
I saw in that imperfect bird
no antipathy, no envy, no vengeance.
It needed no pity,
but just a crumb,
something to hop toward.

A GLOSSARY OF CHICKENS

There should be a word for the way
they look with just one eye, neck bent,
for beetle or worm or strewn grain.
"Gleaning," maybe, between "gizzard"
and "grit." And for the way they run
toward someone they trust, their skirts
hiked, their plump bodies wobbling:
"bobbling," let's call it, inserted
after "blowout" and before "brood."
There should be terms, too, for things
they do not do—like urinate or chew—
but perhaps there already are.
I'd want a word for the way they drink,
head thrown back, throat wriggling,
like an old woman swallowing
a pill; a word beginning with S,
coming after "sex feather" and before "shank."
And one for the sweetness of hens
but not roosters. We think
that by naming we can understand,
as if the tongue were more than muscle.

SLEEPING WITH MY DOG

Even with deer ticks, even with fleas,
even with his snores, breaths
I can't time with mine
in those moments before
both of us fall asleep,
when his back paw begins kicking
like a musician keeping a beat,
and the white of his filmy eye
rises into the night sky of his doggy mind—
even with these, and with the skunky waft
of his silent farts, his dreamy woofs,
which sometimes wake me,
I sleep not really more soundly
but more contentedly
than I would were I alone,
the way a Neanderthal might have,
firelight dancing along a wet wall,
his arm draped over something furred
and warm and respiring not quite in time
with his own life-giving exchange
in some cool and smoky room.

WARREN

Autumn, with its globes, the gold and silver saved,
hanging here and there like something to reach for,
has become this time to walk through

and through which to watch from a distance
seven vultures, like days of the week, turn and turn.
They, too, must be watching.

They must see with keener vision the least leaf
swing upon a stem, a bee visit the sleeping dog.
This is not why they have come.

What the breeze lifts and offers, what the sky accepts
has nothing to do with the orchard, with the dog
in its dream, with you, who can't yet sense

what, between the rows, in a nest of summer grass,
lies strewn like stolen purses. This is why the vultures,
the days of the week come: to assign

a given time a task, to walk, however awkwardly,
toward what the dog has done and what,
when the branches are finally bare,

will waft on cooler air up and down these rows.

PASTORAL

To find such a place,
start with words,
a pantry of birds
edged with fence-
row, scrub trees—
a place
such as this,
glib with the bees'
whispered story
of a wild god
clad in wild phlox,
chicory,
goldenrod
to lead the flocks.

To lead the flocks
through bluets,
through gates
without locks,
find the key
in buttercups,
a map in the arbutus.
Parse the May
apples' spring
lament. Analyze
birch and ash,
saplings
holding hives
above tufts of grass.

Above tufts of grass,
wine-
pink columbine
and white hepaticas,
find antonyms
of anywhere
but here, for here
are the hymns
of idle
days,
saxifrage
and thistle,
hymns in praise
of drooping sedge.

Of drooping sedge;
of the old pasture's
old gestures;
of deerfly and midge,
bluebottle and tick,
chirp if you have
lived
in brick
and stone. Come
to the field,
to the blood-
root and winsome
ginger, the wild
at the edge of an ancient wood.

At the edge of an ancient wood,
the fringed gentians
speak nothing
of their vain pursuit.
Blueberries
hauled
in the filled
bellies
of waxwings announce
no theme
but the old
chance
of seeding again
a better world.

A better world
to remember,
August, September:
the guild
of weed,
passion
fashioned
into seed
without much worry
about time
or death,
though some hurry,
perhaps, some
held breath.

Held, breath
holds nothing else
till nothing tells
it time, then forthwith
it expires,
autonomic,
the way the poem:
it conspires
to take root
and emerge
in an empty space.
So, too,
the urge
to find such a place.

STUPID

Yesterday, out of nowhere,
searching for model ships
on Google, I typed her name
(one I hadn't thought of in years)
into the long white horizon.
And even as I paused at Enter,
a word sailed back to me
as though sifted through
a million pages in the sea
of all my experiences: *stupid.*
"Stupid," I said, and said
again, "stupid." Disyllabic;
a trochee; the consonant blend
of *st*, like part of a stutter,
tongue stuck on palate;
and the long *u*, the way it oozes
off the tip, a glue
to the consonant ending,
itself an accusation.
But who was I accusing?
Her, of being stupid?
Or me for having loved her,
an eighteen-year-old with a kid?
And I thought of my mother,
twenty years younger,
saying to my father,
"How could he be so *stupid*?"
And I wanted to say that the kid
wasn't mine but I liked her,
that both of them were cute
and we weren't being stupid.

But then some other wave
washed over me, and I was back
aboard the *Morgan*
looking for whales,
Googling, typing "model ships,"
or something just as stupid.

TIED DOG

How it must feel to be choked always
at the end of a line,
teeth just out of reach
of whatever's worth snapping at;
to run the rut of hard-packed earth;
to open the throat all day full of faith
in the symbol of a yip, a yelp, a bark.

I watch my neighbor's tied dog,
and it watches me while I wash my car,
mow my lawn, fetch my paper
at the foot of the walk. Now, at my desk,
I stop at the end of another line.
I sigh, I cluck, I grunt.
I look out the window at the panting dog.

LETTER WRITTEN IN POKEBERRY INK

It would likely begin with the salutation
of "Dear" or "Dearest," unless addressed
to a brother back home and so, less formal,
something like "Thomas" or "Lem";
and if a love letter penned before a march
toward some battle rumored to be fierce—
"To My Most Loving Wife." Script, not print,
the writing a bit ragged, as though composed
while hungry or very scared. In spots
where the writer paused—round splotches,
like drips of sweat or blood from a wound
to the head. The content what you might expect—
the rain in Richmond, Chattanooga's
stifling heat, the boredom of the march,
valiant acts only hinted at, memories
of youth, a long untasted dish. In closing,
a compliment, most likely, or an affirmation
of devotion or intent—"Lovingly," "Fondly,"
"Yours," "God Bless." And by the time
it were opened, the pokeberry ink, faded a little
but readable, like scars on skin.

HOMESCHOOLED

Aren't we all, really, in the end?
There's little I remember
from a lecture or a book.
These eggs I know to cook on low,
to swirl around the pan
the way when without a spoon
I stir coffee in a mug.
And with newsprint and a match
how to start the chimney draft.
I see my father strike a blue-tip on his shoe,
my mother shake an omelet onto a plate.
Draped over a clothesline,
a rug can have the dust beaten out of it
with the handle of a broom.
Yesterday I helped a stranded motorist
jump his car. I could hear my father:
red to positive on the dead;
red to positive on the good;
black to negative on the good;
black to grounded metal on the dead.
It's human nature to want to make the dead good.
And sometimes, out of nowhere,
a voice in my head utters the word "nigger."

BABO SPEAKS FROM LIMA

deep memories yield no epitaphs
— Melville

The sun, like a round white bone,
beat our backs—this press borne

westward by the chains of that world
turning and whipped by wind

tattering shrouds furled even against
the broad black shoulders of night—

beat the caulked boards, our bare feet
burning, our wounds salt-stitched and raw;

beat the ocean's eyes to diamonds;
beat down the tiny fishes that leapt in us.

What was it we wore around our
blood and wishes? Some tarred

covering as thin as the inside of a mirror.
Something blue eyes feared for the fear

reflected back at them. Judgments.
Evidence. Drumheads reverberant

with the beat of rowlocks and oars;
beat of the prow crashing toward

that vast, awful, undulating unknown;
beat each of us carried between

our ribs like a thousand nights
alive with legs and firelight, nights

I reclaimed sometimes in the quiet
moments when the firmament,

frozen there in the square of the open hold,
seemed like a sieve through which our untold

protests pulsed. For days I waited.
Watched. When Aranda paced the deck,

my malice followed as close as the famished,
fire-eyed, gale-blasted gulls, which lunged

incessantly at the aft. My head was a hive.
The sea the field of sorghum I'd scythed

before the dry wind blew in from Iberia.
I could no longer remember my daughter,

my wife. I sought them in the women confined
alongside me, and in every eye I spied

a mask I recognized. Night fell as night will fall.
I mined the eyes of Atufal and bade Dago

dig a Spanish grave out of the deep.
How black! How bilious, black, and sweet-

sick blood looks when splashed in moonlight.
I retched at the raw-egg stench of it

the way a boy will to smell a butchered pig.
Death watched, jack-eyed and fettered.

Hatchets dripped. Out of the forecastle
a fowl piped in its ague. All I knew a-keel,

my vision drowned, but come the sun
my purpose swam through the wrack.

I'd yaw even though we'd wreck. I'd barnacle.
O master, I'd try you out to your masts—

fittingly—and my hard heart crash me
back toward home like a figurehead, a figurehead.

SLAVESHIP

There need not be seabirds,
nor even the line-drawn horizon,
the rise of sun or moon.

No colors flapping from a mast,
though, if listened for, closely,
they might be heard,

with gulls keening in their wheeling,
a groaning as of wood stretched
to its lignin, and deeper down

the sound of dragging chains.
Hers is a husband: figurehead
persistently erect.

His a flat, lit screen flickering
big men moving in fits
and starts upon a grid.

Or what they own, which owns them:
tenement, time-share,
mansion, farm.

Maybe yours is a ship in a bottle,
a tipsy middle passage. Or a white
line, like a powdered horn.

Or else it's Internet porn,
day upon hungry day,
a self-sad navigation.

Pinioned by whatever we are,
what we have in common
is the incipient inkling

that, in the shimmering distance,
there may be a wilderness
yet to run through,

a freedom teeming with mosquitoes
for which we'd offer up,
willingly, our naked skin.

MELVILLE PASSING

September 28, 1891

At the very end, his heart
hardly pumping, the long

wake widening behind,
and the white sail bellied,

he didn't think *Ishmael*,
didn't think *Claggart* or *Budd*;

didn't hear the carriage pass
on East Twenty-Sixth,

or the clang of the horse's
one loose shoe; he didn't smell

chestnuts or wood-smoke;
didn't feel autumn slither

beneath the wool; or see
sparks pop in the grate,

or the lamp's wick wink out.
He was watching the sun

sinking into the Great South Sea,
and several houris sprawled

in a cocoa-nut grove,
and beyond a bamboo temple

the tattooed chief sharpening
a blade for the banquet to come.

FIRST PROSPECTIVE

That looking forward—from bloom of youth
to wilt of death—must have, indeed,

tapered, yawning widely at the start with breath
pushed past another's tongue,

musk of tousled sheets on an imagined marriage bed.
Narrowing then, but not much,

with slapping of small feet on a stone floor,
with grins of syrup on a table of oak.

In this *mise-en-scène* neither a stern look
nor a raised hand, neither the grunting weight

nor the plume of a huge cigar. Just a gathering
and focusing of the light of many days.

And all that time ahead like a canker
she could not yet feel, the irritant

necessary to make a pearl, years in the dark.
Or did she know already that marriage

is a lens-bent search for distant objects, their apparent
brightness, nacreous and iridescent,

and that, rising to his requirement,
she'd be looking through a spyglass backwards?

THE COOP

Of what ambitions he had as he neared forty,
having married and found a career, the sort he

thought he'd enjoy, teaching literature to teens,
and his wife not quite the woman of his dreams,

an excess of flesh in their queen-sized bed, his
latest and most passionate aspiration was to raise

chickens. A warm week in February he built
the coop. Fifty yards from the house, atop a hill,

a practical in carpentry, almost level, almost true:
a door, a window, a shingled roof.

He bought the hens from one Farmer Browne,
whose feed store, within the year, burned to the ground

(an incubator light, or so he heard).
They were Golden Comets, the birds,

hybrids with reddish feathers, yellow legs,
wattles like labia majora. He named them

(though he shouldn't have) Martha, Betsy, and Gertrude,
and at dusk that first day, standing in the new coop,

his girls clucking contentedly, the pine shavings
smelling so good and new and not yet full of shit,

he patted each red head, bade adieu,
and left them on their broomstick roost.

It happened not that night but one soon after,
near the end of their marriage but before

she split, that the door was left unlatched,
the plywood board flapping open in the wind

like a restaurant menu, or so he would later imagine.
Better, though, to pretend it happened

the day she left, and that it was her (*feeling what?*),
saying farewell to their hens, for they had no children

(and that was good)—*her* who'd left the door ajar.
Was there a sound in the night, a whimper maybe?

He couldn't be sure. Anyway, when he woke
he must have felt alone enough and so looked

forward to seeing his gals, to gathering the morning's eggs,
brown and still warm, even as he brooded over the empty bed.

It's best he finds them soon after that, all three dead,
scattered throughout the yard in bloody shreds.

DEATH WATCHES

Being, as we are, stuck between
and in the dark, boring, somewhat like them,
through the thick of things, all our lives

scuttling along a track, sucking at pith,
without the art to answer why,
without the beetle's single-mindedness,

it's no wonder we bang our heads,
so to speak, against walls for mates,
conflate the ticking of insect and clock.

Some, they say, lay eggs in books,
whole life-cycles passed in the pages,
story in a story, play within a play.

Once, in an antique shop, I saw a volume
nibbled by larvae, a munched tunnel,
like a space for hiding money or gems.

I, too, have lived in books, some the gifts
of lovers over whose brush-off I scrabbled
toward an unlit and solitary place.

That time's a kind of death, isn't it?
Not just a wounding. A vigil to which
we attend with all our senses—the song

written just for us, a drink wormwood-bitter
to the tongue, ring pulled from a finger,
a lit candle and an opened book.

Not why, then, but when to bite
and what like. My field guide to beetles
says they fancy churches and summer nights.

IN THE BUTTERFLY CONSERVATORY

Quite at home in the brightness
of their own being,
they seemed so unlike the wintered us.
They were a flurry of motley,
fluttering everywhere
like an updraft of sunlit snow.
I felt heavy in my sweater, oppressed
in the humid room.
I wanted to rest against the glass
like the Atlas moth and feel the cool beyond.
There were so many to see it was dizzying.
I watched one, red as an oriflamme,
land on a halved orange,
its proboscis dip into the glistening flesh.
One, the blue of my running shoes,
flapped in the blur beyond my nose,
alit upon my shoulder.
A sign of luck, said some boy.
There must be room for joy,
a door to the other side.

DROSOPHILA MELANOGASTER

Considering what we have to look forward to,
the invasion of our house, of late,

by fruit flies—dark-bellied dew lovers
who criss-cross the shrinking fields

of our vision thinking *banana*, thinking
wedge of orange the way you think

chocolate and I think *sex*—seems less a bother
and more an art, the found kind:

specks of their corpses tiny Rorschachs
in the kitchen sink,

flecks of pepper atop the soap dish soup.
If their incessant transit inches

from our eyes reminds us of refractive defects,
our shared farsightedness, so be it.

I see worse by the week: white crawlies
that trawl across my range of view

when I stand of a sudden or crane my stiff neck;
midlife pimples which, when examined

in the magnified mirror, seem to colonize
like pink mold along my aging brow.

If these fruit flies are drawn to our ripening
flesh, to the pools of our eyes;

if we exude some hint of geriatric tang;
if they want to whelp their young

in our very entropy, should we seek revenge?
We love dew, too, don't we? Sweet juice.

We lick spills. We flit in our futzing.
We fuck and go wash. We're spotting

like these week-old bananas. Our friends are dying
or dead. So, let's not sweat it. Let's not swat.

No bowl of vinegar mixed with liquid soap.
No portable zapper. No sticky ribbons

of fly paper like giant strands of DNA.
Think of Woodworth in his Berkeley home,

doing the dishes, cleaning gunk from the drain,
his breath disturbing their air campaign.

Let's support their art in our employment.
Why overprioritize long-term plans

at the expense of our present enjoyment?

UNCLE

Sometimes they talk with me,
these children I have not fathered,
and the things they say,
though I forget them,
seem like sentences out of books
I read once and haven't thought of since.
Today, a boy who in the absence
of his density might have been me,
the fiddlehead of his hand
in mine, followed me
through the upstairs hall,
asking something which,
if I had to guess,
I'd say had to do with destiny.
Outside, a school bus was passing,
the rev of its engine
like a bow drawn across a string,
a brief life's arc of sound
into and out of the house—
windows and walls and quiet rooms—
where I stood dumbstruck
and almost ready to answer.

ARARAT

Years later, in spite of his weak knees,
he might have labored up that volcanic peak

to gaze upon the giant ribs
of this thing he'd built by hand, the ship

it was sailing into view as through the eyes
of some half-starved songbird looking for a place

to land. And because he'd hewn it,
he might have run his hand along a cubit,

the keel piece bleached as a bone
and smooth, breamed by many days beneath the sun.

There, above the treeline and below the snow,
unsteady on his feet, fatigued, the ship he knew

reduced so, when, at its best
it had quartered all those pairs of beasts,

he would, no doubt, have reeled,
not unlike the Lord seeing his failed

creation. What builder wouldn't glance
between the ruined futtocks and apprehend in the distance

mud structures; smoke of cookfires; shapes
of donkeys, dogs, goats, grazing sheep?

Above the green plateau there is always grief,
which, inspired, becomes the breath of life.

Some Notes

"The Wimp"
Caratunk Wildlife Refuge, owned and operated by the Audubon Society, is located in Seekonk, Massachusetts.

"Luminescent Jellyfish"
The *Charles W. Morgan*, a U.S. whaleship, sailed its maiden voyage in 1841. The world's oldest surviving merchant vessel, it is on exhibit at Mystic Seaport, where it is being restored to seaworthy status.

"Letter Written in Pokeberry Ink"
Pokeberry is the term for the dark purple berry of American pokeweed (*Phtyolacca americana*). Many letters written by soldiers during the American Civil War were composed using improvised ink made from pokeberries when manufactured ink was unavailable.

"Babo Speaks from Lima"
Babo is a character in Herman Melville's antislavery novella *Benito Cereno*, a fictionalized account of a slaveship insurrection, first published serially in *Putnam's Monthly* in 1855. The leader of the slave revolt, Babo was modeled by Melville after Toussaint L'Ouverture, the liberator of Haiti, and is considered by some readers to be the hero of the story. Following his capture, Babo refuses to speak. In Lima, Peru, he is sentenced to death, his head impaled upon a spike.

"Melville Passing"
Melville, relatively unknown at the time of his death, died of heart failure in his home at 104 East 26th Street in New York City on September 28, 1891. According to *The New York Times*, he was "so little known, even by name" that "only one newspaper contained an obituary account of him." Ishmael is the narrator of *Moby Dick*. Claggart and Budd are characters in *Billy Budd*. Houris are Muslim nymphs of Paradise; Melville used this term in his novel *Typee* to describe the women of Polynesia.

"First Prospective"
After Emily Dickinson's "She Rose to His Requirement."

"Death Watches"

The death watch beetle (*Xestobium rufovillosum*) is a wood-boring beetle that gets its name from the ticking sound it makes in order to attract mates. Often heard in old buildings at night, it has become associated with the vigil, or death watch, spent beside the dying or dead. The death watch beetle plays a minor role in Edgar Allan Poe's short story "The Tell-Tale Heart."

"In the Butterfly Conservatory"

The Butterfly Conservatory is a live butterfly habitat housed in the American Museum of Natural History in New York City.

"*Drosophila melanogaster*"

Drosophila melanogaster is the genus and species name of the common fruit fly, also called the vinegar fly. Charles W. Woodworth was an American entomologist and founder of the Entomology Department at the University of California, Berkeley. His study of fruit flies led to breakthrough work in genetics.

"Ararat"

Ararat is a mountain massif in eastern Turkey, near the borders of Iran and Armenia, consisting of Great Ararat and Little Ararat. The former is thought to be the landing place of Noah's ark.

Acknowledgments

Grateful acknowledgments to the following publications, in which these poems appeared previously, sometimes in earlier versions: *Connotation Press: An Online Artifact* ("First Prospective," "One-Legged Pigeon," "Owl Pellet I Show My Students"); *Leviathan: A Journal of Melville Studies* ("Babo Speaks from Lima," "Melville Passing"); *The New Yorker* ("A Glossary of Chickens," "Lot's Wife"); *Ruminate* ("Warren").

I'm grateful to the Arts Horizons Artist/Teacher Institute, Blue Mountain Center, the Fine Arts Work Center, the Geraldine R. Dodge Foundation, Mesa Refuge, the National Endowment for the Humanities, and the New York Foundation for the Arts for the support that made the writing of these poems possible.

Princeton Series of Contemporary Poets